# SRA OPEN COURT READING

# The Wind

A Division of The McGraw·Hill Companies

Columbus, Ohio

## — PROGRAM AUTHORS —

Marilyn Jager Adams

Carl Bereiter

Marlene Scardamalia

Anne McKeough

Marsha Roit

Jan Hirshberg

Gerald H. Treadway, Jr.

Michael Pressley

## Acknowledgements

From GILBERTO AND THE WIND by Marie Hall Ets, copyright © 1963 by Marie Hall Ets, renewed © 1991 by Marjorie M. Johnson. Used by permission of Viking Penguin, an imprint of Penguin Putnam Books for Young Readers, a division of Penguin Putnam Inc. From What Happens When Wind Blows?, by Daphne Butler. Copyright © 1996 by Raintree/Steck-Vaughn Publishers. Reprinted with permission of copyright holder.

## Photo Credits

**24 – 36** © Daphne Butler; **38 – 41** © Daphne Butler; **42** ©Frank Rossotto/The Stock Market; **43, 44** © Daphne Butler; **48 (bl)** © The Bridgeman Art Library.; **48 (r)** © The British Museum, London.; **48 (tl)** © Gift of the W. I. and May T. Mellon Foundation. ©Board of Trustees, National Gallery of Art, Washington DC.

www.sra4kids.com

## SRA/McGraw-Hill

*A Division of The McGraw-Hill Companies*

Send all inquiries to:
SRA/McGraw-Hill
8787 Orion Place
Columbus, OH 43240-4027

Printed in Mexico by RR Donnelley & Sons Company's wholly-owned subsidiary, Impresora Donneco Internacional

ISBN 0-07-569221-X

1 2 3 4 5 6 7 8 9 RRM 05 04 03 02 01

# Table of Contents
## The Wind

**Gilberto and the Wind** . . . . . . . . . . . . . . . . . . . . . . . 4
*by* Marie Hall Ets

**What Happens When Wind Blows?** . . . . . . . . 24
*by* Daphne Butler

**The Wind** . . . . . . . . . . . . . . . . . . . . . . . . . . . . . . . . . . 46
*by* Robert Louis Stevenson

Fine Art . . . . . . . . . . . . . . . . . . . . . . . . . . . . . . . . . . . . 48

# Gilberto
# and the Wind

Marie Hall Ets

*illustrated by Loretta Krupinski*

I hear Wind whispering at the door.
"You-ou-ou," he whispers. "You-ou-ou-ou!"
So I get my balloon, and I run out to play.

At first Wind is gentle and just floats my balloon around in the air. But then, with a jerk, he grabs it away and carries it up to the top of a tree. "Wind! Oh, Wind!" I say. "Blow it back to me! Please!" But he won't. He just laughs and whispers, "You-ou-ou-ou!"

Wind loves to play with the wash on
the line. He blows the pillow slips into
balloons and shakes the sheets and twists
the apron strings.

And he pulls out all the clothespins that he can. Then he tries on the clothes— though he knows they're too small.

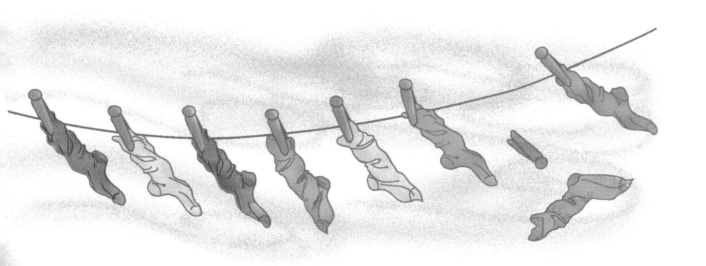

And Wind loves umbrellas. Once
when I took one out in the rain he tried
to take it away from me. And when he
couldn't, he broke it.

If the gate in the pasture is left unlatched, Wind plays with that, too. He opens it up, then bangs it shut, making it squeak and cry. "Wind! Oh, Wind!" I say, and I go and climb on. "Give me a ride!" But with me on it the gate is too heavy. Wind can't move it at all.

When the grass is tall in the meadow
Wind and I like to race. Wind runs
ahead, then comes back and starts over.

But he always wins, because he just runs over the top of the grass and I have to run through it and touch the ground with my feet.

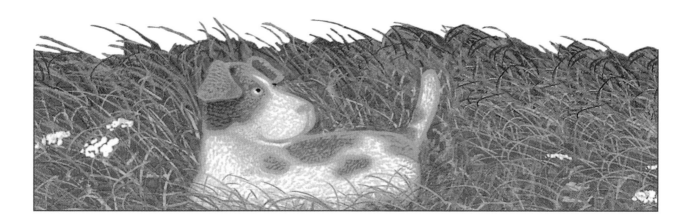

When the big boys on the hill have
kites to fly Wind helps them out. Wind
carries their kites way up to the sky and
all around.

But when I have a kite Wind won't fly it
at all. He just drops it. "Wind! Oh, Wind!"
I say, "I don't like you today!"

When the apples are ripe in the fall, I run with Wind to the pasture and wait under the tree. And Wind always blows one down for me.

And when I have a boat with a paper
sail Wind comes and sails it for me—
just as he sails big sailboats for sailors
on the sea.

And when I have a pinwheel Wind
comes and plays, too. First I blow it
myself to show him how.

Then I hold it out, or hold it up, and Wind blows it for me. And when he blows it, he turns it so fast that it whistles and sings, and all I can see is a blur.

Wind likes my soap bubbles best of
all. *He* can't make the bubbles—*I* have
to do that.

But he carries them way up into the air
for the sun to color. Then he blows some
back and makes me laugh when they burst
in my eyes or on the back of my hand.

When the leaves have fallen off the
trees I like to sweep them into a pile.
But then Wind comes along.

And just to show that he can sweep
without a broom, Wind scatters the leaves
all about again. And he blows the dirt in
my face.

Sometimes Wind is so strong he starts breaking the trees and knocking down fences. Then I'm afraid. I run in the house and lock the door. And when Wind comes howling after me and tries to squeeze in through the keyhole, I tell him, "No!"

But then comes a day when Wind is
all tired out. "Wind," I whisper. "Oh,
Wind! Where are you?" "Sh-sh-sh-sh,"
answers Wind, and he stirs one dry leaf
to show where he is. So I lie down
beside him and we both go to sleep—
under the willow tree.

# What Happens When Wind Blows?

by Daphne Butler

## Wind and Weather

Wind is always changing. It brings
rain, dries the wash, and makes your
ears cold in the winter.

24

Sometimes there is no wind at all.
Other times it's tugging at your clothes
and messing up your hair.

Yet it can blow steadily from one
direction for weeks and weeks.

## No Wind at All

When no wind blows, the air is very still. Smoke, balloons, and bubbles drift slowly upward.

Not a leaf stirs.

## Wind Clouds

High above, thin **wisps** of clouds show that the weather is changing.

Soon a wind will blow. Tomorrow, the sky may be cloudy. Perhaps it will rain.

## A Fresh Breeze

As the wind gets stronger, leaves rustle, and flags wave.

Smoke from chimneys is swept away by the **breeze,** and kites soar in the wind. Sailboats begin to glide through the water.

## Storm Clouds Gather

The wind grows stronger, and dark **storm** clouds gather high up in the air. The ocean forms **peaks,** and the water becomes rough.

On land trees sway, and it is difficult to walk in the wind.

## Dust Storms

Strong winds can lift dust up from the ground. Sometimes, in the afternoon, it seems like it is nighttime.

Fierce winds twist into the air and blow dust upward in a **spiral.** What could happen to you if you were caught in a twisting wind?

## Hurricanes

Sometimes swirling storms form over a warm ocean. They travel toward land and become bigger and faster.

When winds reach 75 miles per hour, the storm is called a **hurricane.**

Another dangerous time to be
outside in the wind is during a **blizzard.**
It's a better idea to stay at home
and keep warm.

## Storm Damage

Strong winds are very powerful. They can destroy crops, blow down trees, and damage buildings. Sometimes people and animals die.

We need to know when a bad storm is on the way. Then we can prepare ourselves for it.

How do we know? Who tells us when a storm is coming?

## Wearing Away at the Rocks

Have you ever been on a beach when the wind has blown the sand against your legs? It stings!

Sand that is picked up by a strong wind hits hard against the rocks. It can make them very smooth. Sometimes it even wears them into strange shapes.

## Power from the Wind

In the past, windmills have used the power of the wind to grind corn and to pump water.

Today's windmills make electricity.
They are silent and clean. All they need
to run is a strong, steady wind.

41

## Air on the Move

The air around the Earth is moving all the time. It moves because the Earth is spinning.

Also, the air moves because parts of the Earth are freezing cold, and parts are very hot.

Air in hot places rises, like the steam from a boiling kettle. Wind blows as more air moves in to fill the space.

## Wind Words

blizzard        A storm with strong winds
                and lots of snow

breeze          A gentle wind

hurricane       A fierce storm with very
                strong winds that travel over
                75 miles per hour

**peaks**    Shapes in the water that resemble the pointed tops of mountains

**spiral**    A shape of a line that winds around a center or point and gradually moves toward or away from it

**storm**    A strong wind that brings rain or snow with it

**wisps**    Thin streaks, usually of clouds or smoke

# The Wind

Robert Louis Stevenson

*illustrated by Lori McElrath-Eslick*

I saw you toss the kites on high
And blow the birds about the sky;
And all around I heard you pass,
Like ladies' skirts across the grass—
O wind, a-blowing all day long,
O wind, that sings so loud a song!

46

I saw the different things you did,
But always you yourself you hid.
I felt you push, I heard you call,
I could not see yourself at all—
O wind, a-blowing all day long,
O wind, that sings so loud a song!

47

## The Wind

*Breezing Up (A Fair Wind).* 1873–1876. **Winslow Homer.** Oil on canvas. $24\frac{1}{8} \times 38\frac{1}{8}$ in. National Gallery of Art, Washington, DC.

*Perspective plan of Venice.* Detail. **Joseph Heintz the Younger.** Museo Correr, Venice.

*A High Wind at Yeigiri.* From the series *Thirty-six Views of Mt. Fuji,* c.1830–1835. **Katsushika Hokusai.** Japanese color print from woodblocks. $10\frac{1}{4} \times 15$ in. British Museum.